STAND UP RIGHT:

Keys to pursue your desires and live a successful life

Lawrence Pate

Table Of Contents

Chapter 1

What The Bible SayAbout Standing Up
100 Bible Verses about
Standing Up

Isaiah 58:1

"Cry resoundingly; let it all out; lift up your voice like a trumpet; pronounce to my kin their offense, to the place of Jacob their transgressions.

Ezekiel 2:1

What's more, he told me, "Child of man, stand on your feet, and I will talk with you."

John 16:33

I have directed these sentiments toward you, that in me you might enjoy harmony. On the planet you will have adversity. However, cheer up; I have beaten the world."

2 Timothy 3:12
To be sure, all who want to carry on with a faithful life in Christ Jesus will be oppressed,
Favored is the one who strolls not in that frame of mind of the devilish, nor holds up traffic of heathens, nor sits in the seat of scoffers;

Ephesians 6:13
Subsequently take up the entire covering of God, that you might have the option to endure in the malevolent day, and having done all, to stand firm.

James 4:17 ESV
So whoever knows the correct thing to do and neglects to make it happen, for him it is sin.

James 5:11 ESV

See, we consider those favored who stayed relentless. You have known about the faithfulness of Job, and you have seen the reason for the Lord, how the Lord is sympathetic and tolerant.

Jews 4:12

For the expression of God is living and dynamic, more keen than any blade that cuts both ways, piercing to the division of soul and of soul, of joints and of marrow, and knowing the contemplations and expectations of the heart.

Galatians 5:1

For opportunity Christ has liberated us; stand firm in this manner, and don't submit again to a burden of servitude.

1 Corinthians 16:13

Be vigilant, stand firm in confidence, carry on like men, be solid.

2 Timothy 3:16
All Scripture is inhaled out by God and productive for educating, for censure, for adjustment, and for preparing in uprightness,

1 Corinthians 15:58
Hence, my adored siblings, be ardent, undaunted, continuously having large amounts crafted by the Lord, realizing that in the Lord your work isn't to no end.

1 Peter 3:15
Yet, in your souls honor Christ the Lord has blessed, continuously being ready to make a guard to anybody who asks you for a justification behind the expectation that is in you; yet do it with tenderness and regard,

Acts 14:10

Said in a boisterous voice, "Stand up standing on your feet." And he jumped up and started strolling.

Disclosure 21:8
However, concerning the fainthearted, the irresolute, the despicable, with respect to killers, the physically unethical, alchemists, misguided worshipers, and all liars, their part will be in the lake that ignites with fire and sulfur, which is the subsequent demise."

1 Corinthians 14:1-40
Seek after affection, and genuinely want the otherworldly gifts, particularly that you might forecast. For one who talks in a tongue talks not to men but rather to God; for nobody figures out him, yet he expresses secrets in the Spirit.
Then again, the person who predicts addresses individuals for their upbuilding and support and encouragement. The person who talks in a tongue develops himself, yet the person who predictions

develops the congregation. Presently I maintain that all of you should talk in tongues, however considerably more to forecast. The person who predicts is more prominent than the person who talks in tongues, except if somebody deciphers, with the goal that the congregation might be developed. ...

2 Corinthians 1:24
Not that we rule over your confidence, however we work with you for your bliss, for you stand firm in your confidence.

Ephesians 6:11

Put all in all protection of God, that you might have the option to remain against the plans of Satan.

Ephesians 6:10

At last, serious areas of strength for being the Lord and in the strength of his strength.

Colossians 2:1-23

For I believe you should know how extraordinary a battle I have for yourself and for those at Laodicea and for all who have not seen me eye to eye, that their hearts might be energized, being weave together enamored, to arrive at all the wealth of full confirmation of understanding and the information on God's secret, which is Christ, in whom are covered up every one of the fortunes of shrewdness and information.

I express this all together that nobody might cheat you with conceivable contentions. For however I am missing in body, yet I am with you in soul, celebrating to see your great request and the solidness of your confidence in Christ. ...

Ephesians 6:10-17

At last, serious areas of strength for being the Lord and in the strength of his strength. Put all in all the defensive layer of God, that you might have the option to remain against the plans of Satan. For we don't wrestle against flesh, however against the rulers, against the specialists, against the vast controls over this current dimness, against the otherworldly powers of detestable in the eminent spots. Hence take up the entire covering of God, that you might have the option to endure in the detestable day, and having done all, to stand firm. Stand consequently, having secured on the belt of truth, and having placed on the breastplate of uprightness, ...

Luke 17:3

Focus on yourselves! On the off chance that your sibling sins, reprimand him, and assuming the stones, excuse him,

Precepts 25:26

Like a ruined spring or a dirtied wellspring is an honest man who gives way before the fiendish.

Favored is the one who strolls not in that frame of mind of the underhanded, nor holds up traffic of miscreants, nor sits in the seat of scoffers; however his pleasure is in the law of the Lord, and on his regulation he reflects constantly. He resembles a tree planted by surges of water that yields its natural product in its season, and its leaf doesn't wilt. In all that he does, he succeeds. The insidious are not in this way, yet resemble refuse that the breeze drives away. Hence the evil won't remain in the judgment, nor delinquents in the assemblage of the equitable; ...

1 Peter 5:9

Oppose him, firm in your confidence, realizing that similar sorts of enduring are being capable by your fraternity all through the world.

James 1:12

Favored is the one who stays undaunted under preliminary, for when he has stood the test he will get the crown of life, which God has vowed to the individuals who love him.

James 1:1-27

James, a worker of God and of the Lord Jesus Christ, To the twelve clans in the Dispersion: Greetings. Count everything happiness, my siblings, when you meet preliminaries of different sorts, for you realize that the testing of your confidence produces faithfulness. Also, let faithfulness make its full difference, that you might be awesome and complete, ailing in nothing. Assuming that any of you needs shrewdness, let him ask God, who gives liberally to all without rebuke, and it will be given to him.

...

Ephesians 4:1-32

I subsequently, a detainee for the Lord, ask you to stroll in a way deserving of the calling to which you have been called, with all lowliness and delicacy, with persistence, holding on for each other in adoration, anxious to keep up with the solidarity of the Spirit in the obligation of harmony. There is one body and one Spirit — similarly as you were called to the one expectation that has a place with your call — one Lord, one confidence, one submersion, ...

Galatians 5:22-25

However, the product of the Spirit is love, happiness, harmony, tolerance, thoughtfulness, goodness, steadfastness, tenderness, restraint; against such things there is no regulation. Also, the people who have a place with Christ Jesus have killed the tissue with its interests and wants. Assuming that we live by the Spirit, let us likewise stroll by the Spirit.

Matthew 5:39

Yet, I tell you, Do not avoid the person who is underhanded. Yet, assuming anybody slaps you on the right cheek, go to him the other too.

Jews 11:1-40

Presently confidence is the affirmation of things expected, the conviction of things not seen. For by it individuals of old accepted their tribute. With a supernatural conviction we comprehend that the universe was made by the expression of God, so what is seen does not consist of things that are apparent. With an otherworldly conviction Abel proposed to God a more OK penance than Cain, through which he was praised as equitable, God recognizing him by tolerating his gifts. Also, through his confidence, however he passed on, he actually talks. Leaning on an unshakable conviction Enoch was taken up so he shouldn't see demise, and he was not found, since God had taken him. Presently before he was taken he was complimented as having satisfied God. ...

Philippians 1:27

Just let your way of life deserve the good news of Christ, so whether I come and see you or am missing, I might know about you that you are standing firm in one soul, with one psyche endeavoring next to each other for the confidence of the gospel,

Acts 15:1-41

In any case, a few men descended from Judea and were showing the siblings,

"Except if you are circumcised by the custom of Moses, you can't be saved." And after Paul and Barnabas had no little dispute and discussion with them, Paul and Barnabas and a portion of the others were designated to go up to Jerusalem to the messengers and the elderly folks about this inquiry. Thus, being sent on their way by the congregation, they went through both Phoenicia and Samaria, depicting exhaustively the transformation of the Gentiles, and gave extraordinary pleasure to every one of the siblings. At the point when they came to Jerusalem, they were invited by the congregation and the missionaries and the older folks, and they proclaimed all that God had finished with them. Yet, a few devotees who had a place with the party of the Pharisees ascended and said, "It is important to circumcise them and to arrange them to keep the law of Moses." ...

2 Corinthians 11:13-15

For such men are misleading messengers, underhanded workers, camouflaging themselves as witnesses of Christ. Furthermore, no big surprise, for even Satan masks himself as a heavenly messenger of light. So it is nothing unexpected if his workers, likewise, mask themselves as workers of exemplary nature. Their end will relate to their deeds.

Romans 15:33

May the God of harmony accompany all of you. So be it.

Romans 12:1-2

I appeal to you subsequently, siblings, by the leniencies of God, to introduce your bodies as a living penance, heavenly and satisfactory to God, which is your otherworldly love. Try not to be adjusted to this world, yet be changed by the recharging of your psyche, that by testing you might recognize what is the desire of God, what is great and adequate and awesome.

1 Timothy 6:12

Stay the course of confidence. Grab hold of the everlasting life to which you were called and about which you made the great admission within the sight of many observers.

Beginning 1:28
What's more, God favored them. What's more, God shared with them, "Be productive and duplicate and fill the earth

Chapter 2

How Do You See Yourself

Seeing yourself as you truly are can be an agonizingly troublesome interaction, however on the off chance that you put the time and exertion into it, meeting your genuine self can be a very compensating experience.

In seeing yourself impartially and truly, you can figure out how to acknowledge yourself and sort out approaches to working on yourself in the Future
Distinguish Your Current Understanding
Work out your perceptions.[1] Pick up a pen and paper and work out a depiction of yourself. Make it as definite as could be expected, characterizing yourself as a general individual: truly, intellectually, inwardly, and profoundly.
Begin with articulations like, "I am..." or "What I'm truly glad for myself for is..."

Answer every assertion with something like 8 to 12 reactions.
List your assets and shortcomings, also. The vast majority can recognize somewhere around something beneficial and something awful about themselves, regardless of how expanded their inner self may be or how whipped their confidence has become. Work out what you accept to be areas of strength for you and your downfalls, as resolved simply by your stomach reaction.

Review huge minutes in your day-to-day existence. Contemplate the tales you habitually share from quite a while ago. Ask yourself what these accounts say regarding you and why you feel a sense of urgency to tell them to individuals you meet.
Focus on what these accounts say regarding you. Do the accounts convey your genuineness or your fortitude? Might it be said that you are enthusiastic about telling them because these attributes embody your standard way of behaving, or do you recount

these accounts since they are uncommon instances of qualities you wish you had a greater amount of?

Recall your young life. A great many people are most genuine to their cravings and character when they are kids. Sort out what fulfilled you as a kid, as well as what left you feeling frustrated. Consider the kind of conviction framework you went by as a youngster. Assuming that a portion of these components has changed, note them, and note the reasons you guarantee behind the change.

For instance, as a youngster, you might have loved the times you spent doing things freely and all alone. On the off chance that you esteem your own space, this desire for opportunity is an undeniable piece of who you truly are.

On the off chance that you are as of now secured to various commitments, however, wonder why. You might have figured out how to esteem loved ones in another manner, in which case, the craving to meet any connected commitments could be important for the genuine you. Then again, you may be connecting yourself down to fit outside assumptions, in which case, the genuine you are as yet the free individual you were as a kid

Prohibit yourself from the mirror.[2] Step away from the mirror for an entire week and quit checking your appearance out. In doing as such, you interfere with any bogus view of your actual self that is constantly kept up with each day when you check what you look like.

Toward the finish of your mirror boycott, you may likewise arrive at the acknowledgment that the only one so concerned and disparaging of your appearance is yourself. When you compel yourself to quit focusing on your alleged actual blemishes, you will probably see that no other person is moving forward to focus on them in your place. Thus, you may ultimately understand that the negative

convictions you held about your appearance are false, all things considered.
Calm the commotion inside your head.[3] Life can be exceptionally requesting and your contemplations can pull you in 100 unique bearings all at once. Work on your life for half a month to assist with limiting the genuine fears and negative self-talk that typically go with a rushed timetable.
On the off chance that you experience issues calming the commotion in your mind immediately, anticipate removing an excursion of sorts from your internal bother somewhat early. Deal with however many of your necessities as could be expected under the circumstances so you will have pretty much nothing, regardless, to do during that week or so of "get-away." Schedule your commitments so there will be no external nerves attacking your contemplations during that time.

Urge others to be completely forthright with you. You want to take a gander at yourself from another vantage point. Somebody who realizes you well is bound to have a decent comprehension of who you truly are, yet interestingly, scarcely any individuals near you will be legitimate, pretty much the entirety of your downfalls. You want to find companions who will be straightforward with you and empower those companions you as of now need to talk to sincerely, unafraid of backfire.

You can make individuals OK with reprimanding you by figuring out how to scrutinize yourself. On the off chance that you can show valuable self-analysis, individuals around you might feel happier with coming clean with you from their perspective.

Certain individuals are normally more OK with telling the truth. Others figure out how to be straightforward once they become OK with somebody. You ought to have either of these kinds of individuals in your day-to-day existence.

At the point when individuals in all actuality do condemn you productively, listen cautiously and acknowledge what they need to say. Try not to respond out of frustration and don't pressure different companions into supporting or denying their cases.

Admire individuals. Individuals disdain to feel unimportant, so generally, an individual who feels seriously about oneself will respond by finding another person who can be peered downward on. However, this mutilates your self-insight. Something superior to do is track down individuals to gaze upward.

Turning upward to others likewise gives you an objective to take a stab at. Nobody is awesome, yet periodically, you will more often than not appreciate individuals who have positive characteristics you tend not to have. Respecting these individuals can make you more mindful of characteristics you don't have, and when you become mindful of these characteristics, you can later take a stab at copying them in your own life Investigate every insight you initially had. After you have given yourself an excursion from your unique arrangement of discernments, haul out the rundown and go through it point by point. Inquire as to whether each direct has any legitimacy toward it and invest the energy cautiously going through the rundown individually. With every insight or proclamation you made, ask yourself:

"Is it truly obvious?"

"Might I at any point demonstrate it to be evident? Might I at any point discredit it?"

"How would I respond, truly and inwardly, to this idea or thought?"

"Are there positive attributes related to this negative quality?"/"Are there negative credits related to this positive quality?"

Break out of your usual range of familiarity. Take a look at your discernment by driving yourself to turn into a fledgling again at something new.[4] During seasons of vulnerability, one's assets and shortcomings are bound to appear on the other side. Give close consideration to your responses during the experience to find out about what your own positive and negative ascribes truly are. Try to find something you don't know anything about and compel yourself into finding out about it. If you don't know anything about cooking, for instance, figure out how to cook.

You want to focus on your reactions and responses during this time. This cycle additionally should be finished all alone. Try not to depend on others to help you through it.

Acknowledge your failings.[5] People disdain being incorrectly, yet no one is awesome. Rather than attempting to deny your downfalls and deficiencies, quit rationalizing yourself and speak the truth about the off-base things. This incorporates the things you previously accepted to be off-base and those you might have recently denied.

Comprehend that tolerating your shortfalls is a vital piece of seeing yourself as you truly are. Besides that, mainly in recognizing and tolerating your downfalls could you at any point desire to develop them in the long run. You want to get rid of reasons, also. For example, assuming you hesitate constantly, don't attempt to legitimize it by saying that you finish the work at any rate thus it doesn't exactly make any difference. All things being equal, basically own up to yourself that you dawdle.

Project deep down. When confronted with inconvenience, search inside for a purpose. It tends to be hugely simple to push the fault on another person, yet to try not to lift your confidence unreasonably, you want to genuinely inquire as to whether you had any issue in the ongoing circumstance, too. Additionally, you ought to project internally at whatever point you feel enticed to whine about others. At the point when this occurs, pause and inquire as to whether there may be others submitting similar questions about you.

Thoroughly search from an external perspective. Contemplate your objectives, thoughts, and wants. You could legitimize and justify everyone in your head, yet ask yourself how you would see these qualities if seeing them in another person rather than yourself. Assuming that the normal response shifts, decide why this is the situation.

For instance, on the off chance that you pine for a relationship with someone in particular and feel supported in your longing, ponder what an outside, an uninvolved individual could see. Assuming a goal view would believe you to be innocent or wild, you ought to attempt to acknowledge that characteristic of yours for what it is.

Keep a diary. Expound on your new disclosures and questions all through the whole course of recharging your mental self-view. You can expound on your sentiments, disappointments, or whatever else is connected with this subject. The important thing is basically to compose reliably and truly.

Each time you plunk down to write in your diary, you ought to continue to compose until you arrive at a comprehension or condition of the uplifted feeling of some kind.

Ensure that you require some investment to write in your diary when you can zero in on the assignment without interruption.

The picture named See Yourself As You Are

Step 147

Ponder yourself in sound ways. While you should speak the truth about your shortfalls, you additionally need to acknowledge yourself for what your identity is and figure out how to speak the truth about your upsides, as well.[6] Having an excessively unfortunate mental self-view can be similarly basically as unsafe as having an excessively expanded mental self-portrait, while possibly not all the more so.

You want to stress to yourself that you are important, even with every one of your issues and shortfalls

At the point when you sense your discernments swinging in an unjustifiably bad bearing, challenge the ridiculous culpability. In the case of something going

Chapter 3

Self Evaluation

The Benefits of Self Evaluation

It may not be obvious to detest discussing ourselves, however, there are many advantages of self-evaluation and appraisal. Frequently assuming you fear your yearly presentation survey, you are in good company. The odds are good that your supervisor is similarly apathetic about the gathering. Various examinations recently have found that supervisors and workers are tired of the yearly act. Organizations are under increasing strain to up their ability executive's endeavors.

The prize discipline design of the yearly audit saps assurance. Directors disdain to lead them and workers fear them. All in all, what's the other option?

Self-assessment and more normal conversations are the new significant and clever approaches to overseeing representative surveys. Lately, many organizations have dumped yearly evaluations for more standard ceaseless input. The development of self-assessment has been a major piece of this shift. Furthermore, presently self-evaluation is demonstrating more fruitful results than the couldn't stand yearly survey.

The accentuation has moved from past execution to what workers need to create and develop. Self-appraisal has been essential to this change.

Need further persuading? Here is the lowdown on the advantages of self-assessment and evaluation.

First up, what's going on here?

What is self-assessment?

Self-assessment is the capacity to look at yourself to figure out the amount of progress you have made. It expects workers to screen their capacities and assess their qualities and shortcomings. It puts representatives to a great extent responsible for their turn of events.

A self-assessment implies considering questions, for example,

self-evaluation where have you succeeded?
What accomplishments would you say you are generally pleased with?
Where do you believe you want more help?
What objectives do you want to have achieved?
What might assist you with achieving these objectives?
What do you most like about your work?
What do you most abhor about your work?

What enhancements could be made to make your job simpler?
Which parts of your occupation might you want to take out and why?
What professional objectives do you desire to achieve in the following three years?
These are the sort of inquiries remembered for a self-assessment - ones that give a brief idea about execution. The motivation behind a self-evaluation is to help a singular know the degree of their capacities and to enhance them. It tends to be overwhelming to a representative when they initially start self-assessing, however over the long run, it turns out to be more regular.

What are the advantages of self-assessment?

Feel more took part in the examination cycle
Acquire more noteworthy experiences and put forth future objectives for development
Have positive expectations about their capacities

Improve limit building (figure out how to rapidly make revisions)
Select preparation programs that generally fit needs
Foster an inquisitive brain for critical thinking
Turn out to be more responsible
Feel more esteemed
Feel more inspired to acquire new abilities
Critically, when representatives feel appreciated through the self-assessment process, they are bound to pay attention to input from their directors. The examination cycle turns out to be substantially more of a two-way conversation when it spins around customary self-assessment.

One of the main parts of self-appraisal to representatives is the independence it gives. The cycle deters micromanagement from group pioneers, which we as a whole know is a smothering channel on efficiency. Representatives who self-assess and are allowed to pursue their own decisions about how they approach their obligations are more joyful, more dedicated, more useful, and more faithful.

Bosses and chiefs benefit significantly from representative self-appraisal.
At the point when a representative self-assesses, chiefs can acquire experiences into how workers feel about their work and how they fit into their group. They can get a genuine feeling of how representatives view their positions. It features misconceptions and workers likewise get criticism from administrators for what spurs them.

It gives entrepreneurs and directors a much more extensive viewpoint to work with and assists them with seeing the representatives' side of the story - it's inescapable that there will be a few distinctions between the perspective of a representative and the individual who oversees them. Yet, numerous good thoughts about how to determine efficiency hitches can emerge from workers.

At the point when chiefs have an unmistakable image of what is most important to a worker, they can boost exclusively to assist each colleague with accomplishing the objectives they have set themselves. It implies chiefs can coordinate errands later on that play to an individual's assets and guarantee preparation and support are set up to address shortcomings.

The greatest advantage for bosses is the certainty it provides for workers. The nonstop course of self-appraisal by workers and resulting individual development is immensely significant to all.

The general advantages of self-assessment and evaluation

The advantages of self-evaluation assessment and assessment self-reflection happen constantly in regular daily existence.

We do this from adolescence - it's how we learn and develop. In training, it is progressively used as an important learning device. As we move into adulthood, the course of self-reflection frequently isn't thought about, yet self-intelligent practices, for example, contemplation and care are turning out to be substantially more typical and are praised by numerous effective business pioneers from one side of the planet to the other.

There's a slight contrast between self-reflection and self-assessment in the working environment, however, the standards are something very similar - everything no doubt revolves around development. While self-appearance in regular day-to-day existence looks for understanding into conduct and values for self-improvement, self-assessment at work is utilized to concentrate on execution to get to the next level

www.ingramcontent.com/pod-product-compliance
Lightning Source LLC
LaVergne TN
LVHW010124170826
845678LV00012B/2578

* 9 7 9 8 8 4 7 4 5 0 4 1 6 *